A Robbie Reader

THREAT TO THE WHOOPING CRANE

Susan Sales Harkins and
William H. Harkins

Mitchell Lane
PUBLISHERS

P.O. Box 196
Hockessin, Delaware 19707
Visit us on the web: www.mitchelllane.com
Comments? email us: mitchelllane@mitchelllane.com

Printing   1   2   3   4   5   6   7   8   9

A Robbie Reader/On the Verge of Extinction: Crisis in the Environment

Frogs in Danger

Polar Bears on the Hudson Bay

The Snows of Kilimanjaro

Threat to Ancient Egyptian Treasures

Threat to Haiti

Threat to the Bengal Tiger

Threat to the Giant Panda

Threat to the Leatherback Turtle

Threat to the Monarch Butterfly

Threat to the Spotted Owl

Threat to the Whooping Crane

Threat to the Yangtze River Dolphin

Library of Congress Cataloging-in-Publication Data

Harkins, Susan Sales.

  Threat to the whooping crane / by Susan Sales Harkins and William H. Harkins.

     p. cm. — (On the verge of extinction)

  "A Robbie Reader."

  Includes bibliographical references and index.

  ISBN 978-1-58415-685-7 (library bound)

  1. Whooping crane—Juvenile literature. 2. Birds—Conservation—Juvenile literature.

3. Endangered species—Juvenile literature. I. Harkins, William H. II. Title.

  QL696.G84H36 2008

  598.3'2—dc22

2008008037

ABOUT THE AUTHORS: Susan and William Harkins live in Kentucky, where they enjoy writing together for children. Susan has written many books for adults and children. William is a history buff. In addition to writing, he is a member of the Air National Guard.

PHOTO CREDITS: Cover, pp. 3, 7, 8, 13—Earl Nottingham/Texas Parks and Wildlife Department; pp. 1, 4, 11, 12, 18, 20, 21, 22, 25, 26, 27—U.S. Department of Interior, U.S. Geological Survey, Patuxent Wildlife Refuge Research Center, Laurel, Maryland; pp. 1 (small picture), 14—International Crane Foundation, Baraboo, Wisconsin.

PLB

TABLE OF CONTENTS

Words in **bold** type can be found in the glossary.

EXTINCTION

All whoopers dance, even the young ones. Nobody knows why, but whoopers seem to dance just for fun!

DANCERS IN THE SKY

In October, **arctic** winds sweep across Canada. The days grow short. In a chilled **marsh**, whooping cranes raise their red heads to greet the cold wind.

It's time to fly south to the warm waters of the Gulf of Mexico. When the wind is strong enough, the huge cranes leap into the air and leave the cold marsh behind.

After many days of flying, the air grows balmy. Gracefully, the cranes glide down to their winter home. The Texas air is calm and the sun is gentle. Whooping cranes feast on crabs, snails, and small fish. With full bellies, they fall asleep under the autumn moon. When they wake, they call softly to one another. *Ker-LOOOOO. Ker-LOOOO.*

A single crane bows its head and flaps its wings. Then it leaps into the air and throws its head back. Its beak reaches for the sky.

Others join the dance. Some dance alone. Some dance in pairs. Sometimes, the whole **flock** dances together.

Across the marsh, red heads bob. Cranes leap and stretch toward the starry sky. White feathers flash in the moonlight. All winter, they eat, rest, and dance.

In April, the whooping cranes fly north to Canada. There, a single crane bows to its mate. The dance begins again. The crane flaps its wings and leaps into the air. Its mate returns the bow, flaps its wings, and runs toward the leaping bird.

When the spring dance is over, the cranes pair off to build nests. For a while, the dancing stops. They are too busy babysitting to dance.

When whoopers are young, they need the right food and plenty of exercise to build strong legs and wings. At five months old, chicks must be strong enough to fly from Canada to Texas.

The chicks spend the summer eating and growing. In late summer, the crane families gather once more. As a group, they begin to bow and leap. The nearly grown chicks flap, jump, and stretch. Soon, the entire flock is bowing, leaping, and stretching. Even before the chicks learn to fly, they learn to dance.

Mmm, crabs! Whooper parents spend their entire day catching food for their chicks. Mom or dad shoves food into the chick's bill. In the wild, the chicks have to swim everywhere because their legs aren't long enough to keep them up out of the water.

WHOOPING CRANE LIFE

Whooping cranes, sometimes called whoopers, spend their days wading in shallow water. Whoopers are **omnivores**. That means they eat plants and animals. They eat insects, fish, crabs, berries, grains, and even small birds.

Like all cranes, whoopers have long, thin legs and necks. Their long beaks are strong enough to crack crab shells. Unlike other waterbirds, whoopers don't have **webbed** feet. Webbed feet are good for swimming, but whoopers don't swim. Their long toes are better for walking in the shallow water.

Three front toes and one small back toe spread out to keep the whooper from sinking into the mud. Long legs keep its feathered body above the water while it hunts for food.

Full-grown whoopers are nearly 5 feet tall. They are the tallest birds in North America. Their wings stretch 7 feet from tip to tip. That's wider than most people are tall. They are thin, weighing between 13 and 16 pounds.

Males are larger than females. Otherwise, adult whoopers look alike. White feathers cover most of their body. A patch of red skin tops their head. Across the front of the face, black feathers blend upward to yellow eyes. Black wing tips can be seen from the ground as the birds fly overhead.

Whoopers mate for life. Each spring the pair builds a nest of sticks, **cattails**, and plants, right in the water. Nearly two feet tall, the nest is high enough to keep the eggs dry. Soon, the female lays two eggs. Both parents

Mom and dad turn the eggs several times a day. While one parent is sitting on the nest, the other will wait nearby or search for food.

take turns sitting on the eggs to keep them warm.

About a month later, a chick taps its **egg tooth** against its shell. It can take hours, but finally, the small reddish brown chick breaks through. The fluffy newborn weighs just 5 ounces. The stronger of the two chicks

eats all the food and grows. The weaker one usually dies.

All summer, the chick eats and grows. By late summer it is almost as large as its parents. Red-brown feathers have replaced its soft baby **down**.

This baby chick is just days old and covered with down. In less than two months, he'll have red and white feathers with black wing tips. When he celebrates his first birthday, he'll be white with a red-and-black crown, just like his parents.

Usually, whoopers live in small family groups. They chase away anything that comes near their home. The male will point his beak upward and trumpet two loud blasts as a warning. Sometimes the female joins him. Her call is higher and shorter. The noise can be heard for over a mile. In fact, the

The whooper's call is louder than any other crane's. Whoopers make many different sounds, including a unison (YOO-nih-sun) call that they make with their mate.

whooping crane is named for its loud trumpeting call.

Hidden loops in the whooper's throat are the secret to its loud voice. Stretched out, these coils are about 52 inches long. That's almost as long as the bird is tall!

EXTINCTION

The young whooper, on the right, is nearly grown. In the wild, young whoopers walk a lot while searching for food. That helps their legs grow strong and straight. In captivity, people must take the chicks walking or swimming to make sure they get enough exercise.

DELICATE BALANCE

Whoopers eat a lot. An adult whooper can eat more than a pound of grain each day, so they need a lot of space. A pair of wild whoopers can claim nearly 300 acres. That's a lot of land for just two birds.

Whoopers are picky about their homes. They like wetlands. Wetlands are areas where there is more water than dry land. Sometimes, people drain wetlands to build homes and grow crops. When that happens, the whoopers die. Whoopers need wetlands to live.

Whoopers spend each summer in Canada. In autumn, before their marshes freeze, they fly 2,500 miles south. In Texas, wetlands stay warm all winter. In early spring, the whoopers fly back to Canada to raise a new chick.

Migrating whoopers follow the same **flyway**, or route, that whoopers have flown for thousands of years. Some days, the whoopers fly 300 miles. During their trip, they must stop to rest and to eat. No ordinary field will do. They must find a marsh or pond, or keep flying. Many wetlands along their flyway have disappeared. From the sky, the birds see only farms, houses, and roads. Without places to rest and eat, some whoopers don't survive.

The trip to Texas is harder on young whoopers than the adults. They aren't used to flying yet. They need to take plenty of breaks along the way.

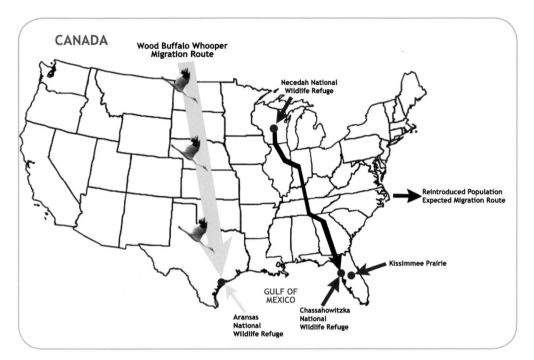

CANADA
Wood Buffalo Whooper
Migration Route

Necedah National
Wildlife Refuge

Reintroduced Population
Expected Migration Route

Kissimmee Prairie

GULF OF
MEXICO

Chassahowitzka
National
Wildlife Refuge

Aransas
National
Wildlife Refuge

Today's largest flock of wild whoopers still migrates between Canada and Texas. The trip takes several weeks. When whoopers are raised by biologists in Michigan and then freed, they will likely be trained to migrate to Florida. The whoopers in Kissimmee Prairie are a resident flock. They do not migrate.

People must protect wetlands for the whoopers. If the wetlands disappear, wild whoopers will also disappear.

Adult whoopers have bright yellow-gold
eyes. Until a whooper is six months old, its
eyes are blue. The leg bands help biologists
keep track of the birds.

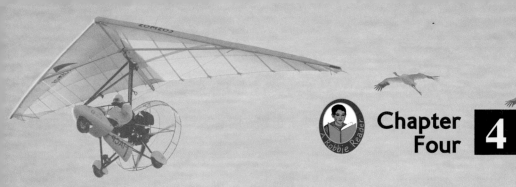

THE PEOPLE FACTOR

Scientists believe whoopers were on earth before people. At that time, the land was wet. Whoopers had plenty of food. There were no people to count them, but evidence shows there were hundreds of thousands of whoopers.

The land began to dry out about 20,000 years ago. Whoopers don't do well on dry land. Some of them stopped laying eggs. Mother Nature was the first to put whoopers at risk.

About 300 years ago, people started moving west through North America. Settlers passed through Iowa, Illinois, Minnesota, and North Dakota, where whoopers lived. Some people stayed in the Midwest. They drained the wetlands for farmland. Many whoopers lost their homes.

Patuxent Wildlife Research Center raises chicks from eggs. Laz, the female in the background, hatched from an egg laid at the center. Alta, the male, hatched from an egg taken from the wild.

Some hunters ate whoopers and stole their eggs. In 1890, a whooper skin sold for $18. An egg sold for $2. Farmers shot the birds as they flew over their farms. The farmers didn't want the whoopers to eat their grain.

By 1900, there was only one small flock left. They nested in Wood Buffalo National

Wood Buffalo National Park in Canada is a seasonal home to many whoopers. Whoopers roost at night in deep water to keep themselves safe from predators, such as the bobcat.

Park in Canada and spent winters on the Blackjack Peninsula in Texas.

President Franklin D. Roosevelt turned the Texas marsh into a **refuge** in 1937. He named it Aransas National Wildlife Refuge. Protecting the whooping crane's winter home still wasn't enough. Many died when they flew into power lines along their flyway. In 1942, only 16 whoopers were left in the wild. Was it too late to save the whoopers?

EXTINCTION

Scientists wear special gear to feed the chicks they raise. The suit is white, like an adult crane's feathers. The hand guard used to feed the chicks looks like an adult crane's head.

PAST SOLUTIONS AND FUTURE HOPES

In the early 1960s, a **biologist** named Ray Erickson tried something new. He took a few eggs from the wild and raised the chicks in **captivity**.

Erickson knew the whoopers would become **extinct** without people's help. He convinced the United States government to pass the Endangered Species Preservation Act in 1966. This act protects **native** plants and animals at risk. Now it is against the law to hunt whoopers or to steal their eggs.

Americans and Canadians worked together to save the whoopers. Like Erickson, they took one of the two eggs from wild nests and raised the chicks at Patuxent Wildlife Research Center in Laurel, Maryland. At first, many chicks died. Now, most chicks grow into healthy adults. Thanks to this program, we know what whoopers need to grow into healthy adults. Unfortunately, these whoopers aren't wild or free. They live in protected pens. People feed them and keep them safe.

Biologists tried to create a wild flock by putting whooper eggs in the nests of sandhill cranes. The whoopers hatched and grew, but they didn't mate. The experiment failed to produce more wild whoopers.

The Patuxent center started a new **resident flock** in Florida in the 1990s. The biologists released captive whoopers into a protected, but wild, area. These whoopers are wild, and they live in Florida year round.

Biologists also tried to create a new wild migrating flock. The biggest problem was

Tux was born in captivity at the Patuxent Wildlife Research Center. When Tux was about seven months old, he was released into the wild in Florida.

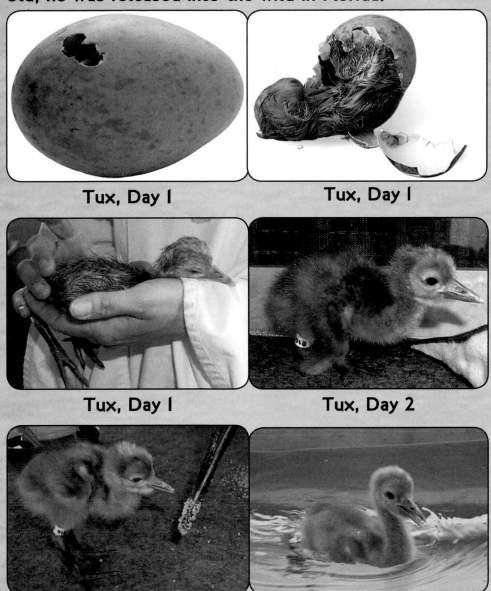

Tux, Day 1

Tux, Day 1

Tux, Day 1

Tux, Day 2

Tux, Day 3

Tux, Day 9

teaching captive chicks how to migrate. In 1997, Kent Clegg led a flock of captive whoopers from Grays Lake, Idaho, to Bosque

A sandhill crane keeps the egg of a whooping crane warm. Whooper eggs vary from soft blue to olive green or tan. They usually have tan and brown spots, which help hide them from predators.

Year	Number of Wild Whooping Cranes in North America
1940	22
1950	34
1960	33
1970	56
1980	76
1990	146
2007	360*

*This number doesn't include the 84 chicks born in the spring of 2007 in Canada.

del Apache National Wildlife Refuge in New Mexico. He flew a small aircraft and the whoopers followed him! In 2007, the program was still teaching whoopers how to migrate.

Brooke Pennypacker used an ultralight aircraft in 2004 to teach whoopers how to migrate. The 1,200-mile trip took 64 days.

During the last week of 2007, two cranes were spotted in Nashville, Tennessee. They had been hatched in captivity and taught to migrate from Wisconsin to Florida. Now they are migrating on their own.

2007 Flock Totals

Flock	Adults	Young	Total	Adult Pairs
Wisconsin Migratory Flock	55	28	83	4
Aransas/Wood Buffalo Wild Population	236	Unknown*	236+	69
Florida Resident Flock	40	I	4I	I7

*84 chicks hatched in Wood Buffalo in spring 2007. Experts expected about 50 juveniles to reach their winter home in Aransas.

In 2008, there were 360 wild migrating whoopers. Another I49 were living in captivity. Whoopers will survive in the wild only if people maintain wetlands along their flyway and protect their nesting grounds.

Captive Programs	Number of Captive Cranes in 2007
Patuxent Wildlife Research Center, Maryland	63
International Crane Foundation, Wisconsin	36
Devonian Wildlife Conservancy Center, Calgary, Canada	23
Species Survival Center, Louisiana	8
San Antonio Zoo, Texas	8
Calgary Zoo, Alberta, Canada	2
New Orleans Zoo, Louisiana	2
Homosassa Springs Wildlife State Park, Florida	2
Lowry Park Zoo, Florida	2
Jacksonville Zoo, Florida	2
Milwaukee County Zoo, Wisconsin	I
TOTAL	**I49**

WHAT YOU CAN DO

Whooping cranes aren't out of danger. They may always need our protection. As long as their **habitats** are in danger, the cranes are in danger. Working together, people must protect remaining wetlands. There are several things you can do to help the whooping cranes.

- Learn more about whooping cranes. We must know what they need so that we can provide it.
- Talk about cranes. The more people know and care about the whooping cranes, the more people will work to protect their flocks, flyways, and homes.
- Volunteer at a National Wildlife Refuge or other wetlands sanctuary in your area.
- Make your yard friendly to wildlife.
- If you're lucky enough to see whooping cranes, don't disturb them.
- If you find an injured whooping crane, report it to your local game warden.
- Write to government agencies and conservation groups. Let them know that you want to help protect the whooping cranes.

Aransas National Wildlife Refuge
P.O. Box 100
Austwell, TX 77950

Canadian Nature Federation
85 Albert Street
Suite 900
Ottawa, Ontario
KIP 6A4
Canada

International Crane Foundation
E-11376 Shady Lane Road
Baraboo, WI 53913

Nature Conservancy Canada
110 Eglinton Avenue, West
Suite 400
Toronto, Ontario
M4R 1A3
Canada

United States Fish and Wildlife Service
1849 C Street NW
Washington, D.C. 20240

Wildlife Diversity Program
Texas Parks and Wildlife
4200 Smith School Road
Austin, TX 78744

Whooping Crane Conservation Association
715 Earl Drive
Lawrenceburg, TN 38464

Wood Buffalo National Park
Box 38
Fort Chipewyan, AB
TOP 1B0
Canada

Books

Goodman, Susan E. *Saving the Whooping Crane.* Minneapolis, Minnesota: Millbrook Press, 2007.

Spinelli, Eileen. *Song for the Whooping Crane.* Grand Rapids, Michigan: Eerdmans Books for Young Readers, 2000.

Theodorou, Rod. *Whooping Crane.* Chicago: Heinemann Library, 2001.

Works Consulted

Allen, Robert Porter. *The Whooping Crane.* New York: National Audubon Society, 1952.

Baur, Donald C., and William Robert Irvin. *Endangered Species Act: Law, Policy, and Perspectives.* Chicago: American Bar Association, 2002.

Bergman, Charles. *Wild Echoes.* New York: McGraw-Hill Publishing Company, 1990.

Chase, Alston. *In a Dark Wood.* New Brunswick, New Jersey: Transaction Publishers, 2001.

Doughty, Robin W. *Return of the Whooping Crane.* Austin: University of Texas Press, 1989.

Ellis, Richard. *No Turning Back: The Life and Death of Animal Species.* New York: HarperCollins Publishers, 2004.

McNulty, Faith. *The Whooping Crane: The Bird That Defies Extinction.* New York: E.P. Dutton & Co., Inc., 1966.

Meine, Curt D., and George W. Archibald (compiled by). *The Cranes.* Gland, Switzerland: IUCH Publications Services Unit, 1996.

On the Internet

International Crane Foundation
http://www.savingcranes.org/

Journey North
http://www.learner.org/jnorth/search/Crane.html

National Wildlife Federation; Central Platte
http://www.nwf.org/centralplatte/

Operation Migration
http://www.operationmigration.org/

Texas Parks and Wildlife
http://www.tpwd.state.tx.us/huntwild/wild/species/?o=whooper

U.S. Fish and Wildlife Service; Aransas National Wildlife Refuge
http://www.fws.gov/southwest/REFUGES/texas/aransas/whoopingcranes.html

U.S. Fish and Wildlife Service; Whooping Crane
http://www.fws.gov/endangered/i/B0F.html

Whooping Crane Central
http://har.scdsb.on.ca/mblack/whoopers/

Whooping Crane Conservation Association
http://www.whoopingcrane.com/

Whooping Crane Eastern Partnership
http://www.bringbackthecranes.org

Wood Buffalo National Park
http://www.pc.gc.ca/pn-np/nt/woodbuffalo/index_E.asp

arctic (ARK-tik)—From the area near the North Pole.

biologist (by-AH-luh-jist)—A scientist who studies living things.

captivity (kap-TIH-vih-tee)—Kept by people instead of living in the wild.

cattail (KAA-tayl)—A tall reed plant that grows in water.

down (DOUN)—The soft fluffy protective feathers on baby birds.

egg tooth (EGG TOOTH)—A small rough knob on a chick's beak that the chick uses to break open its egg.

extinct (ik-STINKT)—A species that is gone forever.

flock (FLOK)—A group of birds that live together.

flyway (FLY-way)—The route a flock of migratory birds takes when moving from winter to summer grounds and back again.

habitat (HAA-bih-tat)—The type of area in which an animal usually lives.

marsh (MARSH)—A swamplike area where there is more water than dry land.

migrating (MY-gray-ting)—Moving from one home to another at regular times.

native (NAY-tiv)—Living things that grow and live naturally in an area.

omnivore (OM-nuh-vor)—An animal that eats both plants and animals.

refuge (REF-yooj)—A safe and protected place.

resident flock (REZ-uh-dunt FLOK)—A group of birds that stays in the same area all year long; they don't migrate.

webbed (WEBD)—Having flaps of skin growing between the toes to aid in swimming.